The Book of Flowers

by Delilah McCrea

The Book of Flowers
by Delilah McCrea

©2024 by Delilah McCrea

dtmccrea.wordpress.com

Pumpernickel House Publishing
Pumpernickelhousepublishing.com

Published in the United States of America.

All Rights Reserved.

No part of this book may be reproduced in any form or by any electronic or mechanical means, including information storage and retrieval systems, without express written permission from the author, except for the use of brief quotations in reviews.

This is a creative work. All characters, places, and incidents are products of the author's imagination. Any resemblance to real people or current events is purely coincidental.

Cover art by Xuan Loc Xuan
instagram.com/xuanlocxuan

For Dad

Contents

I
A Map to the Moon   3
Self-Portrait as a Boy   5
Sentimental Poem Ending with a Suicide   6
A Tired King Constructs a Shopping Mall That Is Filled with Existence 7
Today I Put on My Favorite Outfit so I Could Feel Terrified   9
I Write Entirely Too Much About Blood   10
On Occasion of My Own Death   12
The Moon Is Reading the Communist Manifesto in a Labyrinth   13
Alula   14
O Patron (Saint) of the Drive-thru Window   15
Elegy to Bees   16

II
Created Myth   20
Hematidrosis   22
A Poet Listens to a Harp That Plays the Music of Optimism   23
A Poem Made Entirely of Questions   24
It's Easier to Write Poetry About Dead Things   26
Every Day I Eat One Cloud from the Sky   27
The Republic of The Great Pacific Garbage Patch   28
Soil   29
I Never Write About Desire   30
Every Day I Wake Up and I'm Still in Hell   31
You discover that you are a prime number in human form   34
Imagine a Bladeless Knife With No Handle   35

III
February in Ohio 39
Elegy for Those Still Living   40
Doubt   41
How My Father Did Not Say Goodbye   42
A Professor of English Literature Finds Out That She Does Not Exist   43
A Trumpet Suddenly Appears Beside You. A Nun Says: "This is the End."   44
I Admire the Betta Fish Because I Too Am Beautiful and Want to Fight Everything   45
All My Organs are Paper Mache   46
Maybe You're the Only One Who's Flown a Rocketship to the Moon   48
The Summer I Didn't Kill Myself (and Every Summer Since) 49
In the future I will live on the moon 51
In Which I Give My Father a Bouquet of Delphinium   52
(or A Poem to My Dad, Instead of About Him)   52

IV

The Gospel According to My 3am Drunk Texts   57
All of My Poems Are Prayers   58
Poem in Which I Answer the Questions   60
A Queen passes a Law Against Consciousness   61
Friend,   62
There Is a Tulip in the Garden of Eden That Feels Clean.   63
You Asked Me the Meaning of Life 64
I Prefer Metaphors to Similes Because I Prefer to Say What a Thing Is   65
My Mother Sends Me a Picture of My Dead Father Holding My Brother and I   66
When I Receive the Email of My Pushcart Nomination Immediately After My Zoom Call with My Psychiatrist   67
Nothing in This Poem is True   68
A Poet Steals the End of the World and Hides It Inside a Cathedral   69

Acknowledgements   70
About the Author   73

I

A Map to the Moon

Walk from here to the center
of the Sonoran Desert.

There is a pale blue house
on fire.

This is not yet the center.
Walk past it.

Walk past the roadrunner
nest in the prickly pear

in front of the burning house.
Walk past the anemone tuberosa

and the centaurium calycosum.
Walk past the kit fox with

the kangaroo rat in its jaws.
Walk past the coyote

with the kit fox in its jaws.
Walk past the shed rattler skin.

Walk past the sound of the rattle.
Walk past the heap of your

own shed skin.
Walk past the coyote

with your blood on its chin.
There is a solitary picnic table

off of interstate 8.
Walk another twenty feet

past that. Feel the mountains
holding you,

the saguaros watching you,
older than you can comprehend.

Kneel here.
Cup your hands and wait

for rain that will not come.
Drink the water that fills your hands.

It is sweet.

Self-Portrait as a Boy

I paint a field of forget-me-nots
and in that field
no one is lying,
and in the space where no one is lying
you come and kneel.

You dig your fingers
into soil and wrap them around roots.

You excavate the earth
in the shape of no one, and then
you cut open your belly and remove your insides.

You cradle each bloody organ in your arms
kiss them all on their non-existent foreheads
and place them gently in the ground.

Then you weep.

You weep for what has spilled from you.

Weep for what you have buried here

in the grave of my
flowers,

in the grave
of my weeds.

Sentimental Poem Ending with a Suicide

I think it happened like this
I was lying alone
in a field of daisies
tasting my own blood
but
maybe
you sent me a shoebox
with six daisies inside
I opened my mouth
and placed the stems in the vase
of my throat

I think it happened like this
you were driving to Portland
somewhere in flyover country
you pulled over and ran
into a field of daisies
and never came back
but
maybe
I bought you a bouquet of daisies
from the store beneath your apartment
I walked home
and set them on fire

I think it happened like this
I was a daisy
you plucked me and breathed me in
for ten minutes straight
then you went home
and swallowed every pill in your house

A Tired King Constructs a Shopping Mall That Is Filled with Existence

You and I are there. We are on the display rack in the window of the Footlocker. We are sitting next to each other with our knees pulled to our chests and our feet extended outward on the ground in front of us. We are wearing sneakers, and we are trying to make our bodies look like sneakers, like a pair. We are holding hands. You, in this case, are the reader. You, the reader, and I, the poet, are here in the tired king's shopping mall filled with existence. We are holding hands, and looking at ourselves through the window of the footlocker holding hands and trying to look like sneakers. God is here too. You say *I want to see God*. I say *don't we all*. You say *don't be pedantic. You know that's why we came here*. It's true. When the tired king built his shopping mall filled with existence that's how he drew everyone in. *Come to my shopping mall filled with existence and see God*. The statue of the horse outside of the P.F. Chang's by the front entrance has a banner on it that reads, simply *INSIDE: GOD*. You and I saw an infomercial for it. A middle-aged man with shiny teeth and hair and a bad suit said *If you want to see God go to the shopping mall and buy my book*. Or perhaps that was a televangelist program. Perhaps the infomercial said only I am that am. You say *I came here to see God but we've only seen ourselves*. So, we start walking down the hallway that ends at the entrance of the JC Penney, which is also a Dillard's, which is also a Macy's, which is also a Kohl's. We can already see from where we are that the only thing inside the JC Penney Dillard's Macy's Kohl's is the entire moon. We pass the Spencer's and inside its door is a blackhole. We pass a PacSun and inside its door is a barren, cracked desert landscape with a single golden suncup blooming at the center. The last store in this hall is a Hot Topic. Everyone is there. Everyone is shopping at Hot Topic and everyone is also working at Hot Topic and everyone is also on display at Hot Topic. Everyone's bodies are mannequins for t-shirts and everyone's bodies are also on display to be sold. Everyone is buying each other and themselves. Everyone is selling each other and themselves to each other and themselves. We are there in all of the same roles as everyone else. We both consider buying Nirvana t-shirts and then decide we shouldn't. Instead you buy gauges and I buy a pronoun pin. We still haven't seen God. So, we head back towards the food court. As we pass the Kay Jewelers at the corner you nudge me and so I approach the man at the counter. *Um excuse me*, I say *we were wondering if you could tell us where we might find God? God is here*. He says, without gesturing toward anything. You, the reader, are becoming frustrated. *Make him say something else*. You say. *Um, I'm sorry, where is here, exactly?* I say. *God is here*. He says.

Today I Put on My Favorite Outfit so I Could Feel Terrified

bleed me
bleed me
bleed me

a grapefruit

as bitter juice
drips from chins

of every passerby
and I

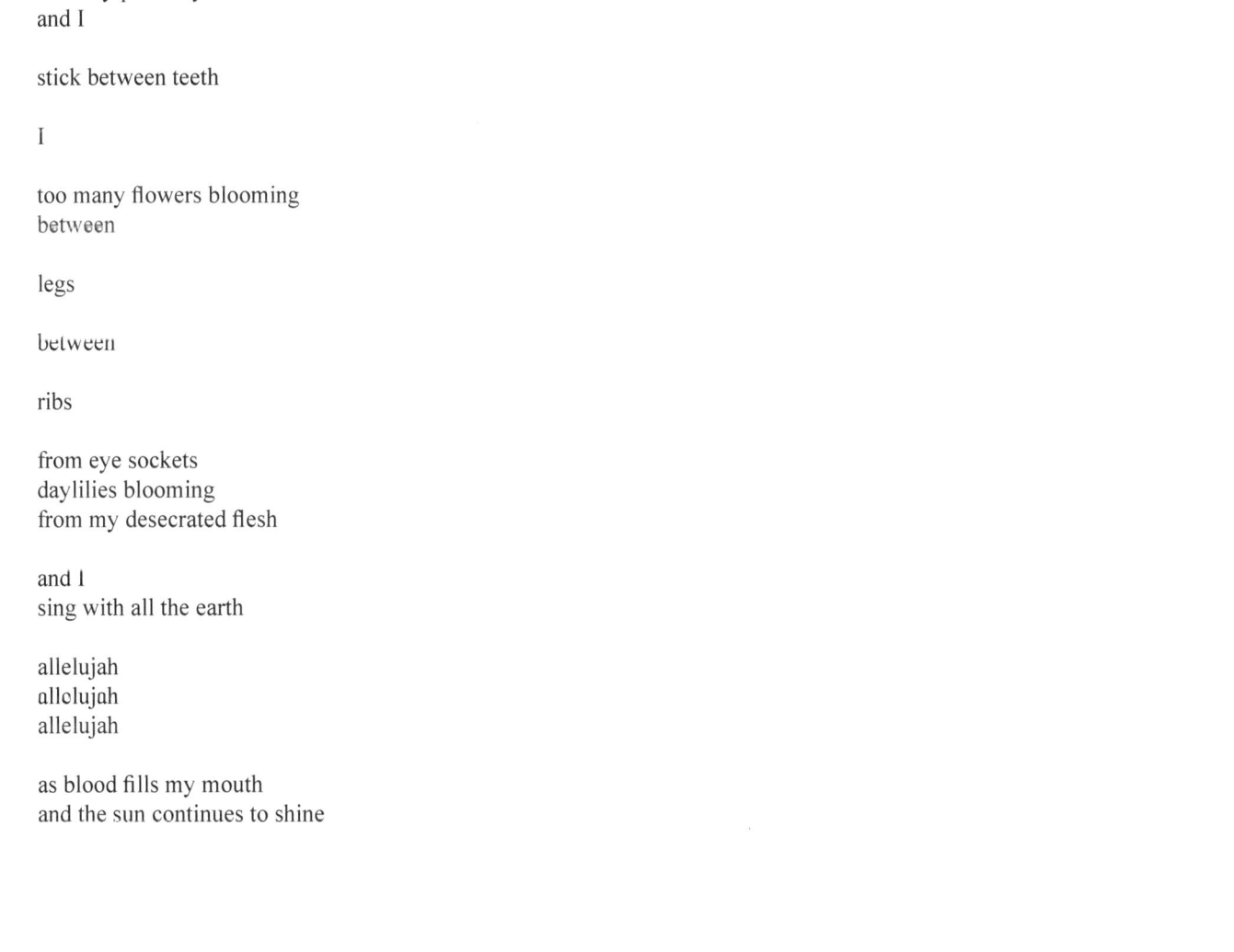

stick between teeth

I

too many flowers blooming
between

legs

between

ribs

from eye sockets
daylilies blooming
from my desecrated flesh

and I
sing with all the earth

allelujah
allelujah
allelujah

as blood fills my mouth
and the sun continues to shine

I Write Entirely Too Much About Blood

instead i'll write about wine
grapefruits
pomegranate

sacrament

sunbursts
and solar flares spilling
from my flesh

carnations
blooming from my wrists

the truth is

i've never made myself bleed

not because i'm squeamish
but i didn't want to leave

a mark

didn't want anyone
to ask

if i'm okay

On Occasion of My Own Death

Please read this poem as I walk into the ocean.
Don't read it on the beach with a crowd of listeners
I don't want to make a spectacle.

You will know when it is happening.
You will have a dream with many broken things:

a clock
a zippo lighter
seven snapped human femurs laid at your feet.

In this dream a cardinal will be perched in the windowsill
demanding repentance.
It will hold in its left talon a daffodil.
This will signify nothing.

When you awaken from this dream
this poem will be sitting on your lap.
Someone will hand you a glass of water
and when you look up you will see thirty folding chairs arranged at the foot of your bed
occupied by eleven people.

When you finish reading the crowd will say

What a beautiful poem.
What does it mean?

and you will drink from the glass of water.

The Moon Is Reading the Communist Manifesto in a Labyrinth

and I am drinking sixty-dollar whiskey, alone
in my four-hundred-dollar apartment.

Everyone walking outside has a mouth
full of posies.

They are singing, but no one
can hear them.

They are too kind.
Their kindness is untenable.

I try to love them
with my cynicism,

but they just keep
dying right there in the street.

I am a hole
inside of a hole.

I tell them it is okay,
they can go home and rest,

but they just keep singing.
They pull the posies from their mouths

and fill me with them.

Alula

In a dream
you don't know me.
Don't know who I am now.

I see you lying pale in your bed,
my mother screaming over your body
gnashing her teeth.

I see myself.
A boy, hollowed
haunting the space outside your bedroom door.

The house dissolves
into the sand.
I wander 22 miles to the heart of the Sonoran Desert.

Angel's trumpets
blossom their song
my sweet liaison.

I eat them all, whole.
Every bird in the desert
swallows me in a murmuration.

They cover me
with their bastard wings.
You are my father.

I am not your son.
How I long
that you will still call me child.

O Patron (Saint) of the Drive-thru Window

please tell me to smile more. It almost gives me gender euphoria, being patron(ized) like a woman by someone who certainly doesn't see me as such—my opal flower piercing removed, my long purple hair tucked under my official McDonald's Brand ™ baseball cap, which I wear backwards when I'm working the closing shift with the Chill Manager ™ so I can feel a bit more like a tomboy. Oh boy do I love explaining to the angry soccer mom that the Pikachu her daughter received is not, in fact, *a boy's toy* and that we are only currently carrying Pokémon in all of our Happy Meals™. I'm surprised this lady isn't objecting to the general demonic nature of Pocket Monsters. How many times have you been handed a biblical tract by a customer at your job? I once received one that was a comic in which the final panel featured the disembodied voice of God telling the main character (as it were) *It's too late to apologize now* over, presumably, the flames of hell (this is, of course, a true story). I may not smile much ever nor have a very convincing Customer Service Voice™, but I'm also the only employee at this particular McDonald's (managers included) to never get in a screaming match with a hostile customer, which seems to me a pretty fair trade for my corporate overlords. Though, they aren't exactly in the business of fair trades. Unless you consider exchanging one's will to live for $8.25 an hour fair. I don't have it so bad though. Sure, I have to walk 2.3 miles over hilly roads to work and back every day. And sure, in the winter I make this walk while wearing two fall jackets and no gloves. And sure, every time I make this walk I consider hurling myself off the bridge to the train tracks below. But hey, at least I have a BA in philosophy. And at least I'm only feeding my own mouth with that $8.25. And at least I split my rent three ways. And at least when Ronald McDonald himself walked in our store and unloaded an AR-15 on me and all my coworkers it was only a dream. Or was it a fantasy? This is no longer a poem. It's a direct letter to you , Ronald. I'm begging you, grant me the sweet mercy of death. Hang me from a cross in the parking lot like one of those three guys I saw in a picture on Facebook. This is a real picture. You can see it for yourself. Just google *McDonald's Crucifixion*, then walk into your garden, and weep.

Elegy to Bees

I used to write poems about dying
now I write poems about flowers
blooming
which I think means

I'm closer to death

write what you know
they say, but I think we write what we're drawn to
what feels farthest away
most unattainable

what does it mean
to be alive
in a dying world

to open oneself

what does it mean
to be a field of sunflowers
and watch
as every bee on earth
falls from the sky

II

Created Myth
After Mathias Svalina

In the beginning God wondered
where everything that wasn't

there yet came from, but
God couldn't think of a good explanation

so they just proclaimed *I did it.*
And the first human asked *When?*

And God said *Just now.*
And the first human became

aware of themself and
instantly got a terrible headache

and said *Ow. Jesus. Why would this exist?*
And God said *You just need some ibuprofen*

And the first human said *Oh yeah,* but then
they remembered ibuprofen didn't exist yet,

and also that they weren't supposed to be a human yet.
Just as they were turning back into a singularity

a melody got stuck in their head. The one
that was playing in the grocery store earlier.

The annoyingly catchy one that the first human
was ashamed to admit they liked.

They racked their brain to remember the lyrics
but their brain wasn't there because they

were a singularity now.
So, then they expanded

into hydrogen and helium and
all kinds of other elements and

stars and planets and
all kinds of living organisms

and then they became aware of themselves again
and decided they liked being called human.

This time there were a lot of them
and they would get cold and hungry sometimes.

And sometimes when they saw each other
cold and hungry, they would wrap each other

in blankets and make each other soup,
but sometimes they wouldn't help each other

at all. They'd just say *you should work harder*
as they ate food grown by their underpaid employees

on land they inherited after their great grandparents
stole it from someone else.

And sometimes the first human who was cold and hungry
would get so angry at the first human who was hoarding wealth

that they would spend all day fantasizing about beating
them to death. They would get so angry they'd forget

to drink water. Forget to love themselves.
Forget about the time their partner surprised them

on a Wednesday night with a bouquet of their favorite flower—
pansies—and some Chinese takeout. Forget about how

for a few hours they both pretended the rent wasn't due
the next morning, and binged *The Good Place* on Netflix

and made love and fell asleep on the couch.
After all that forgetting the first human

fell to their knees and cried out God
I feel so lost and confused, please

help me remember.
And God said

This is the story of a girl
who cried a river and drowned the whole world

and while she looks so sad in photographs
I absolutely love her

Hematidrosis

God planted that garden
in gethsemane and used you as the fertilizer.
& I wish I could tell you I've felt what you felt then,
so sure of what must happen that blood seeped through your pores,
but I've never been certain of anything.

> I think of the butch lesbian pastor I once knew
> who—when she was still a Catholic nun—had a vision
> of you bleeding on a cross
> & how you told her being gay wasn't a sin
> but doubting was.

& the dream I had
where you reached out your hand to show me
the wound, still gaping and bleeding
& when I reached out to touch it
a rose burst from the hole & it smelled
just like the ones on the bush my mother grew
by our mobile home in Arizona.
& how it begged me to believe this was real.

> But I never once
> smelled those roses at my childhood home.

A Poet Listens to a Harp That Plays the Music of Optimism

It doesn't sound like wind
blowing through a field of lilacs.
It sounds like every precinct in this city
burning to the ground.
It sounds like shattering glass.
It sounds like thousands of voices crying out
fuck the police!
It sounds like rinsing
tear gas from someone's eyes.
It sounds like decapitating
a statue of christopher columbus.
It sounds like decapitating
christopher columbus.
It sounds like a riot,
which sounds like love.

A Poem Made Entirely of Questions

I

A swan is eating another swan.
It is not beautiful.
It is hideous, and bloody, and terrifying.

It is also beautiful.

II

Your mother goes to the doctor and they find
a shadow on her lung.
When they open her up, inside
her lung is a blossomed calendula.

When the doctors ask
how it got there she says
she inhaled it whole, on purpose
wanted it inside her ribcage.

When they ask why
she says *I didn't want
the shadow to be
a tumor.*

III

Alone at 2 am
in the kitchen you hold
a knife to your wrist.
Later, you don't.
There is no blood, no scars.

You smoke a cigarette
on your back porch
and look up at the moon.

IV

Inside of God's mouth
there are many rows of teeth
like a shark.

This thought brings you no comfort.
Because of this,
you know it is true.

V

VI

Blue whales can live to be
one thousand years old, if
we all want it enough.

VII

Every morning, as soon
as you awaken your arms
are outstretched, palms facing
heavenward

pooling with blood.

VIII

Here is a gun.
Here are seven violets.
Here is a collection of black and white
photographs of telephone poles.
Here are all of my baby teeth.

It's Easier to Write Poetry About Dead Things

because I can tell myself I'm breathing
new life into them.

Instead of sacrificing that which is already breathing
at the altar of the static image.

But my images aren't static. If you put down
a book of my poems, it will be empty

when you come back. The words so full of
life they ran right off the page, marching

through your house, breaking windows
and setting little fires in your shoes.

You know what they say;
you can never read the same poem twice.

I read that in a poem once, and when I read it again
it said the same thing.

I could say *If I find some petunias in the wild*
cut them from their roots, and give them to you

we call that romance
but it's a trite criticism.

Whoever *we* is, we know
that the real love is in the after.

Is in the *you* putting water in a vase
trying—for a short time—

to keep alive
these dead things you've been handed.

Every Day I Eat One Cloud from the Sky

I am trying
to open the heavens

I am trying
to fill my mouth with sin, so I may speak to God

Or to the sun
and ask it—humbly—not to burn us anymore

to pretend there are still clouds
pretend there are no holes in the sky

Or I'll say to ~~God~~ (the sun)
I am a lamb('s-ear), fill me with your ~~wrath~~ (rays)

so that
~~the others shall live~~ (I may bloom)

The Republic of The Great Pacific Garbage Patch

The Mayor called a meeting and said *We must do something about the sea turtles.* You see, their coastline was made of mostly six-pack rings and commercial fishing nets. So now it was made of mostly dead sea turtles with their necks caught in six pack rings and commercial fishing nets. The Mayor's aid suggested they build a monument from the turtles, said their settlement needed some art. The treasurer said they could build a giant cross like that one in Texas. The chief of police said *we're twice the size of Texas, let's build one twice as big!* So, they ripped up the coastline and stacked all the sea turtles into a cross. Think of a number that's big enough to shock, but still feels real when you hear it. That's how many turtles are in that cross. And in the shadow of that cross stands the First Baptist Church of GPGP, built from the carcass of a Pizza Hut. They tried to say the building had always been a church, but everyone knows what a Pizza Hut looks like. On the first Sunday of every month inside that rotting Pizza Hut they take communion. First, they dip their Styrofoam cups in the pools of blood at their feet and drink. (There are pools of blood all over the Garbage Patch. No one knows where all the blood comes from, and also they know exactly where it comes from.) Then, they eat the discarded plastic sleeves of saltine crackers. Every time, the pastor chuckles and says *Our flesh is already full of plastic anyway* and then someone in the back of the church tears their robes and weeps. Then the whole congregation will get in their cars—mostly '09 Chevy Cobalts—and drive down the street to Hamburger Hill for brunch. Hamburger Hill is the cute nickname the townies gave to the restaurant district. It's also a literal small mountain made of empty Big Mac boxes and McDouble wrappers. On top of that hill sits the signs to every fast-food chain you've heard of. It's just the signs though, there's no restaurants, and no food. The customers drive up to their chosen sign and yell their orders up to dutiful employees sitting on top, who then spit down into the customers waiting mouths. After brunch the churchgoers drive home to their Amazon box houses and enjoy an afternoon of family time watching VHS tapes of 90s Cowboys' games. One Sunday a young boy who didn't like football took a stroll in his backyard and found an unopen bag of sunflower seeds. He ripped the bag open with delight and quickly planted one of the seeds, but nothing grew because the yard was made of plastic.

Soil

death is a doorway

not for me
but from me

& what more
could I aspire to
than soil
than earth

with every flower
I can name
rooted in my body
how could I possibly
be wasted

I Never Write About Desire

by which, of course,
I mean sex.

It's not a conscious choice,
I'm just preoccupied with death.

Perhaps this is why I'm bad
at sex, bad at living

at wanting to.
I only write of mouths

when they're filling
with blood, lips only

busted, or blue and cold
hands only ever gripping

knives. The only warm and wet
I can imagine is a wound

carved in my own wrist.
My lilacs are only metaphors

for corpses. This is an excuse
of course. The real reason is

I do not occupy my body.
Have not, since before I can

remember. You see, I want
so desperately, to touch

God, but I do not want
to be touched.

Every Day I Wake Up and I'm Still in Hell

No matter how much I drink.
The pills aren't helping either.

My doctor says I need
to give them time. Maybe

I need to up the dose,
take them all at once.

Please don't
read this poem

as a cry for help.
This is not

a cry for help.
Please

do not

help me.
Please.

Sorry. I know you're expecting
more poem shit: The body,

crumbling. God,
somewhere. Blood

in mouths or palms,
rendered somehow artistic,

beautiful. The flowers,
always the flowers.

If you turn the page
there's a pressed daisy waiting for you.

You discover that you are a prime number in human form

while counting the petals of a marigold

0
      1
           1
                 2
                      3
                           5
                               8
                                   13

seventeen
years since you stopped breathing

                                               3am text message
                              your friend across the country tells you
                                  they're on acid at a hardcore show
                 says they feel more like a math equation than a person

you wonder if you ever felt
like a person

                0
                     1
                         1
                             2
                                 1
                                    1
                                       0

                                            or is it twenty-one
                                         years without breath
                             twenty-one years since you first realized
                                             you were alone

Imagine a Bladeless Knife With No Handle
After Kaveh Akbar

Imagine yourself
        unable to imagine
                yourself.
Now imagine a bladeless
        god with no handle
—no handhold,
just sharp edges
        that aren't there
                slicing open your
reaching palm. Imagine
        blood leaking from a
                wound in your poem(

)Imagine
                                              a petalless
                                        rose with no stem
                                          gripped in the open-
                                          lipped smile of
                                  my toothless mouth.
                                              Imagine me
                                    squeezing your hand
                          with my nonhand
                                              beckoning
                                          you to where
                                  you're imagining

III

February in Ohio

It's been a mild winter. Nonetheless I've spent it mostly indoors,
mostly lying awake in my bed until noon.

Still trying to call my depression seasonal,
blame it on the position of the earth and the sun,

instead of chemicals in my brain or
a whole continent on fire, or children in cages,

or how I just read that the US government blew up an ancient indigenous burial ground
housed inside of a protected national monument

two hours from where I grew up in Arizona
to make room for this country's ultimate monument to white supremacy.

No, it's just seasonal. And today, what brief January ice that came has already thawed.
So I put on my favorite spring jacket and go for a walk. Feel the sun on my face, it feels so close.

A few blocks from my house I find a cluster of Virginia Bluebells. Some have bloomed into their
cornflower blue trumpets, some are still in rose-pink buds. I think about how flowers

could be any color, how nature could be monochrome.
Instead we have all these shades. Overhead I see hundreds of swallows suddenly fill the air.

I think about how we live on a planet where we can see hundreds of tiny, feathered creatures
dancing against a bright blue sky,

how we have all of this,
how this is all we have.

Elegy for Those Still Living

you're still standing there, a little girl in the desert,
your house buried by a sandstorm seventeen years ago.
& two thousand and twelve miles away every green thing
has turned to ash, turned to a smoldering carcass, turned to rubber
fumes. fumes that seeded themselves in your grandfather's lungs
like so many dandelions. the way ceramic fumes would fill your
father's lungs and sear holes in his flesh, in his pancreas,
like the two thousand and twelve mile hole seared in the sky,
just big enough for the sun to force its way through
and burn down everything you've ever touched.
& is this a poem about your dead father or
about the dying world. & you're not sure
there's a difference.

Doubt

The day I stopped believing in God
I planted seven bleeding hearts
around your grave.

When they bloomed I walked
through their archways
into your open mouth.

In the cavern of your throat
I watched the stone be rolled away
and from the empty space of your ribcage
arose the words

I love you
I love you
I love you

How My Father Did Not Say Goodbye

I walked home one day at eight years old
to find, in the plot of Arizona desert where my house once stood, nothing
but my father planting one hundred cardinal flowers.

No Dad, I said
they won't grow here.
It's too dry.
I know, he said.

Then he knelt down
and kissed me on my forehead
and every flower awoke at once.
A river was flowing from their base.

Look son, look at the mountains.
Your mother is there. She is waiting for you.

I turned but saw only the mountains
being swallowed by the sun.
When I turned back
my father was shoulder deep in the river
descending as though walking on a staircase.
Just as the last inch of him submerged
the river dried up, and the cardinals turned to ash.

In their place one hundred saguaros grew.
I cut down the smallest one, and drank from it.

A Professor of English Literature Finds Out That She Does Not Exist

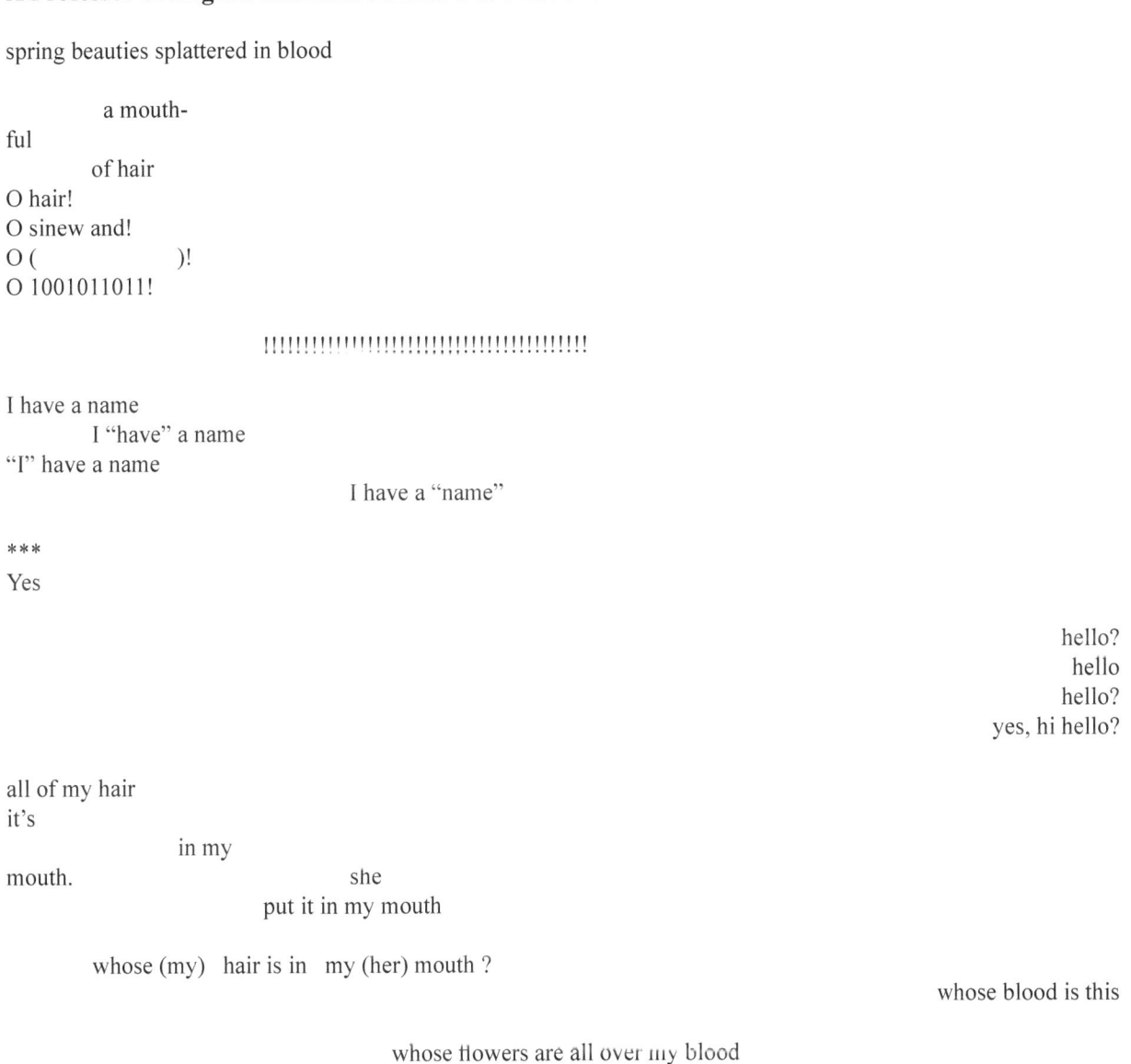

spring beauties splattered in blood

        a mouth-
ful
        of hair
O hair!
O sinew and!
O (   )!
O 1001011011!

                      !!

I have a name
        I "have" a name
"I" have a name
                          I have a "name"

***
Yes

                                                          hello?
                                                          hello
                                                          hello?
                                                     yes, hi hello?

all of my hair
it's
                in my
mouth.   she
                    put it in my mouth

        whose (my) hair is in my (her) mouth ?
                                                                   whose blood is this

                    whose flowers are all over my blood

A Trumpet Suddenly Appears Beside You. A Nun Says: "This is the End."

but the sky does not open up.
Outside your window
a cherry blossom blooms.
You feel a warm hand on your shoulder.
Someone in another place
is crying.
You know
where you are going.

I Admire the Betta Fish Because I Too Am Beautiful and Want to Fight Everything

I think this as I watch Myself smoke a cigarette with blood dripping from her nose. Myself and I are both catching our breath between rounds of a friendly bareknuckle boxing match. We are in our makeshift corners—leaning against a Subaru Forester and Chevy Cavalier respectively—in the dirt parking lot behind the local punk bar. It's 3am and no one is out here with us except God. All three of them—Father, Son, and Holy Spirit—have front row seats to our fight. Before we started, they all placed bets but when I asked Jesus who they each bet on he just knelt down and started drawing in the dirt. I looked at God and said *your son's a weirdo*, then Myself and I both chuckled as we made our way to our corners. Now we're emerging for round three and she's got blood stains down the front of her black crop top and my fishnet sleeve is torn at the elbow. We both have each other's black lipstick on our knuckles. As we get in striking distance I think *this is just like that one scene in Fight Club* except we're both real, and we're both me, and David Fincher and Chuck Palahniuk can both get fucked with their semi-ironic celebrations of toxic masculinity. There's no masculinity to be found here. Just two girls, who are one girl, beating the shit out of each other for fun. I throw a right hook that lands hard against her jaw but just as I connect she hits me with a leg kick. My knee buckles and she takes the opportunity to bust my mouth with a straight right. I taste the sweet iron of my own blood. She tries to follow up quickly with a roundhouse to my head but I back up just in time. As she stumbles from the missed kick I tackle her to the ground. We wrestle for awhile until I end up on top of her in full mount. I start raining down punches against her arms raised to cover her face. Behind her blocks I hear her start laughing, and I start laughing, and she takes the opportunity to roll me over and now she's on top inside of my guard. She grabs both of my wrists and pins them above my head. We're still laughing with our faces inches apart when she kisses me on the lips. I flip her over and I'm on top again but in a position more like loving than fighting. I see a dandelion on the ground by her head so I pluck it and tuck it behind her ear. Then I slide down into the crook of her arm and lay my head on her chest. We sync our heavy breathing together. The night air is crisp and stings against our bare skin. It feels good. It feels like we're alive.

All My Organs are Paper Mache

That's why I spend an hour
on the toilet every morning.

My dentist thinks, I drink too
many acidic beverages.

I don't have a dentist,
but I do have cavities.

I fill them with
baby's-breath &

cigarette smoke.
The paper

of my skin is all
obituaries.

All the same obituary.
My father's.

My father collected every newspaper
from every city in the united states

for every day he was alive.
Then he found his own obituary in each of them.

He cut the obituaries out crumpled them
and began throwing them at

the empty space I was standing in.
They didn't fall to the ground and

build into a pile of me. Rather
they stuck and levitated in the air

throughout random spots of
my empty body. My mother

provided the paste with
tears and spit.

They told my brother
they were building him

a volcano for the science fair.

He cheered and cheered with

every new wad of me
that collected, until

I stood, fully formed &
blinking.

When does it explode?
My brother asked

just as my father erupted.

Maybe You're the Only One Who's Flown a Rocketship to the Moon

this velvet
universe will always
bleed
fire
to transform us
into
ghosts
into
peace
into
broken windows
into
a specific bird
into
a seven-car pile-up
into
this poem
into
nothing
into
naked children
running through a field of hydrangea

The Summer I Didn't Kill Myself (and Every Summer Since)

I want this to be a hopeful poem, but that summer
is this summer

and it isn't over yet. No matter what happens
know that I love you. No matter what happens

know that I'm trying. Every day
I tell myself

that there's still some things I haven't done
that might be worth doing,

still some bands I haven't seen live,
still some friends I haven't danced with.

It's harder now. I don't know when
I'll get to do those things again.

But I'm still trying, and no matter what
saguaros will still be covered in flowers come spring

and that's something.
One year, as hard or harder than this one,

I went camping for my birthday. And I don't like camping
but it was my friend's birthday too, and I like her

and I liked her sister even more. So, I went camping
and I walked alone into the woods and read

What It Looks Like To Us and the Words We Use by Ada Limón
and started sobbing. And I don't know what that means

but it means something to me.
I hold onto that, on nights like this.

Nights like this are most nights
some years and some nights every year,

but tomorrow I'm gonna wake up and I'll still be here
and I don't know what that means

but it means something.

In the future I will live on the moon

I will sit in a crater as my throne
a crown of four o'clocks upon my head.

When I am thirsty
I will imagine oceans

blue
as they used to be

as I stare out
at the burning, black earth.

When I am lonely
I will imagine I am not lonely.

I will pull seeds from my pockets
and scatter them on the rocky surface.

I will imagine them growing
covering my kingdom in green.

When I long to
hurl myself into the sun

I will imagine that my body
is already radiant,

imagine
that I can feel warmth.

In Which I Give My Father a Bouquet of Delphinium
(or A Poem to My Dad, Instead of About Him)

It was in a dream last night.
I gave him the flowers and then we hugged

until I woke up.
It's not true.

I've only dreamt of him once,
and he felt cold and distant in a way

he never did when I was a boy.
But yesterday was his birthday,

and I may not have given him flowers
but when mom told me what day it was

I did have a cigarette under the moon and say
Heres to you dad. Not because he smoked,

but because he's dead.

//

I'm sorry dad.
This was supposed to be to you

but here I am talking like you're not
in the room again.

I don't know if you'd like flowers,
but I know you liked soft things.

I know you filled our childhood room
with stuffed animals even though we were boys.

And maybe it's just because
you were so damn good at the claw machine

but you don't get good at the claw machine
unless you want stuffed animals.

What I'm trying to say, Dad
is I love you.

What I'm really trying to say, Dad
is I hope you still love me.

I hope where ever you are that you can understand
in a way I doubt you would if you were still here.

I hope if I see you again
that you'll call me by whatever name I ask.

But see Dad, I kept the D and the T
because I'd never want to lose your initials.

What I'm really trying to say is
it hurts so goddamn much,

and I don't know whether there's
a you to write to anymore.

Anywhere.
But there has to be.

What I'm really trying to say, Dad
is I miss you.

IV

The Gospel According to My 3am Drunk Texts

In the beginning was the Word and the Word was as of yet undefined. The Word had freckles across the bridge of her nose that only showed up in the sunshine, and the freckles were complemented really nicely by the shade of pink she'd just dyed her hair. In the beginning the Word was God and the Word was with God—they were roommates. The Word had met God through a Craigslist ad. She was moving to the west coast to get an MA in sound design at a small arts college—even though she couldn't really afford it, because damnit she loved making music and she was good at it and she wanted a couple years to dedicate to it—and God had just dropped out of that same arts college after his best friend (and lead singer of his band) OD'd and he was too depressed to finish school, so now he needed a new roommate to split rent. She liked that he was plugged into the local DIY scene, plus he seemed like a nice enough guy—even though he was as bro-y as you'd expect the bassist in an all-dude punk band to be, and he wasn't really one for deep conversations—but they'd have late night Smash Bros sessions on his Switch after he'd close up at the bar and it was fun and it felt kind of like he was the older brother she never had. And she was pretty sure he'd clocked her right away—she could just tell—but he never said anything or asked any invasive questions. And then one night when she ran home crying—because she'd been walking back from the corner store in her favorite leather miniskirt when some asshole yelled *faggot* and threw a bottle at her out of a passing car—God asked her what was wrong, and if he should call off his shift, and she told him no, because neither of them could miss a paycheck if they were gonna pay rent this month so he went to work. Then after binging a few episodes of Steven Universe and crying all night she noticed God was later than usual, and when he finally got home he had a bouquet of daylilies and some lipstick in her favorite shade of purple that he picked up from the Walgreens down the street. And when he gave them to her she started crying all over again and he held her in a way that said this wasn't romantic because he knew she wasn't into guys and he respected that, he just cared about her. And if you haven't figured it out by now in this poem The Word is Jesus and Jesus is a trans girl and her roommate, God, loves her. And she's beautiful, and she's just figuring out who she is as a person and what she wants to do with her life. And she looks just like me, if I looked just the way I want to.

All of My Poems Are Prayers

that's why I couldn't
tell you what
they mean.

My tongue falls
out of my
mouth and slithers
away.

I ask God
to teach me sign
language in sign
language I
invented.

God answers with
a phone
call from the
hospital.
Mom's there again.

I bleed into
the receiver the
nurse says she'll
transfer me
to the cancer
ward.

An old
man I've
never met tells
me he's hungry and
they'll only feed him
Jell-O, cries. The line
goes dead.

When I can't hear
God anymore I
swim out to the great
pacific garbage
patch and plant easter
lilies in my garden there.

Then I enter
the cabin I
built from empty

2-liter bottles of Dr.
Thunder and read
my holy scriptures:

a grocery list in my dead
father's hand
writing, every
item crossed
out.

Poem in Which I Answer the Questions

Why do I insist
there is beauty in death?

Are my mother's lungs
not filled with air?

Where is God
in this poem?

Where are the flowers?
My father?

Does my father have to be
in every poem I write?

Why would I ask a question
I already know the answer to?

Do I want to live
forever?

Why would I want to live
forever?

Can you hear me?

A Queen passes a Law Against Consciousness

You are sitting on a park bench
reading the Gospel of Thomas

using an iris for a bookmark.
I am lying in the field before you

looking at the sky and reciting
the shapes of the clouds:

fig trees
a cockroach
your childhood home
what I can remember of my father's face
forgiveness
the Nicene Creed

Fat droplets splash on the pages
of your book one by one.

My face is suddenly wet. We're both
laughing as tears stream down our cheeks.

In the distance some boys
chase a rabbit. One of them holds

a large stick. The boys surround
the rabbit who freezes in fear,

the boy breaks the large stick over
his knee, and the rabbit flees.

You are holding me now or
I am holding you, a sudden

bundle of arms and torsos
and words

I'msorryIforgiveyouIloveyouI'msorryIforgiveyouIloveyouI'msorryIforgiveyouIloveyouI'msorryIforgiveyouIloveyouI'msorryIforgiveyouIloveyouI'msorryIforgiveyouIloveyouI

Friend,

It was a beautiful planet.
It smelled always of soil
which smells something like
the desire to keep breathing.

Every inch of it
was covered in
tiger lilies.
Not exactly every inch,
but that's how it feels now.

So many birds filled the sky
that if they wanted to
they could have blotted out the sun,
but they never wanted to.
They only danced in its rays.

It was a beautiful planet.
That's all that matters now.

Friend,
you must remember
it was a beautiful planet,
and we lived there once.

There Is a Tulip in the Garden of Eden That Feels Clean.

How we all did, once.
When we stood before God

naked and aware of our nakedness.
Yes, aware. You see the story

gets it wrong. Shame comes not
from knowledge, but from forgetting.

Forgetting that when you stand dripping
in front of your bathroom mirror

after a shower
God is looking at you and

you are looking
at God.

You Asked Me the Meaning of Life

I opened my mouth to answer
but it filled with peonies
they kept coming and coming
cascading out of my mouth
and piling around my feet.

You picked one up and smelled it.
Of course, you said, *it's so simple.*

I tried to tell you I was choking
in sign language
but then I remembered
that I don't know ASL and besides
my hands had turned into vines
wrapping themselves around nearby trees.

The peonies kept coming
piling up to my waist now, still climbing.
My legs weren't even there anymore
it was just peonies.
As they reached my chest
I tried to scream for help
with my eyes, but my eyes turned
to soil and poured out of the sockets.

I felt your hand cup my cheek.
Heard you, choking back tears, say

Thank you, thank you.
You were always a dear friend.

I Prefer Metaphors to Similes Because I Prefer to Say What a Thing Is

death is death is death is death is
death is death is death is death is
death is death is death is death is
death is death is death is death is
death is death is death is death is
death is death is death is death is
death is death is death is death is
death is death is death is death is
death is death is death is death is
death is death is death is death is

do my obsessions count as poetry

that's for you to decide
dear reader

or it's not
I can't decide

let's start over

death is a half-peeled blood orange on a kitchen table
not the suggestion of the absence of the one who never finished peeling the orange
but the orange itself
the raw red fruit staining the wood
death is there
somewhere
I think

let's start over

death is not an orange blossom
but it smells like one
if you want it to
or it doesn't

I can't decide

let's start over

death is

My Mother Sends Me a Picture of My Dead Father Holding My Brother and I

She finds the picture while unpacking
a box of dragons.

I see the text just as I'm headed to Walgreens
for my prescription of escitalopram.

Later, my dear friend messages me wanting to know
if my psychiatrist is taking new patients.

Later, my mother tells me my cousin has died.
She fell on some steps and her brain hemorrhaged.

Later, I imagine what that might feel like
rubbing my fingers on the back of my head in the shower.

Later, I stare at myself in the mirror for seventeen minutes.
Later, my gums bleed as I brush my teeth. I watch the blood,

go down the drain and imagine I spit it up from my lungs.
Later, as I lie awake in bed I feel a sharp pain in my lower back.

I imagine my father's pancreas—rotted and cancerous—in my body.
Later, I'm back in the shower rubbing my fingers against my head again.

I feel a soft spot in my skull, press against it, and my fingers slip through.
I expect viscera, but instead I feel something delicate and velvet-like.

I begin coughing and walk from the shower to the sink.
I hack something up and when I look down to see it the sink is full of rose petals.

I feel that sharp pain in my back again.
I grab my phone and look at the picture my mother sent.

We all look so happy.

When I Receive the Email of My Pushcart Nomination Immediately After My Zoom Call with My Psychiatrist

I burst into tears.
Mom tells me she knows Dad is proud of me too—
wherever he is.
Then she calls me her son.

Life is like this.

It makes a river of you
and you flow into the ocean.
The ocean is terrifying
and it is also full of garbage,
but at the bottom of the ocean—
in some places—
there are meadows of seagrass,
and these meadows bloom with flowers,
and it looks like the world
after the flood
still being the world.

Nothing in This Poem is True

Not even that declaration of untruth.

Look, I am trying to be honest with you
but I need you to trust me.

Stop reading this poem.

Go out to your garden
(you have a garden—trust me).
There you will find a solitary
flower which you did not plant—
a flower that reminds you of the person
whom you most and least want to be reminded of
(this is always the same person—trust me).

Do you see the flower? Good.
Now, I want you to pick it.
Trust me.

Have you picked the flower? Yes?

Why would you pick the flower?

They planted it in your garden just for you.
That flower belongs in your garden.
Your missing person belongs in your garden.
Where else would they be, now that they aren't here?

You should not have picked the flower.
You must now make amends.

Go find another garden that belongs to someone you don't know.
Trust me.

You need to plant a flower in this stranger's garden.
No, not that flower you just picked. That's your flower.
You must plant a flower that will remind this stranger
of the person they most and least want to be reminded of
(always the same person).
You will know what flower to plant when you get to the garden.
Trust me.
Have you found the garden?
And did you plant the flower?
The right one?

A Poet Steals the End of the World and Hides It Inside a Cathedral

Everyone inside the cathedral is smoking cigarettes—Marlboro 27's. A sad song that sounds happy is playing, and someone says they wish somebody would make a happy song that sounds sad. Everyone mutters in agreement, but no one really wishes for that. The end of the world is not so much hidden as it is stored. No one knows what it looks like or where it is exactly, but they know it's inside of this cathedral, and the closed doors are the only thing keeping it there. It's like Schrödinger's apocalypse. Most of the conversation is about the end of the world, trying to guess which object it is among them. Some children run around the stage playing a game in which they touch each item declaring it the end of the world. The pulpit is the end of the world. The organ is the end of the world. The poinsettia. The stained glass. Quickly this devolves into a game of tag, the children chasing each other and declaring *You're the end of the world! No, You're the end of the world!* Inside of the confessional booth a philosophy student is typing a dissertation on the infinite, she thinks to herself *When I finish this paper, it will surely be the end of the world*. In the basement a group of people are watching a movie projected against the wall. It's one of those films where many things happen and none of them move a plot forward, but you can tell this is an intentional choice so you admire it rather than deride it. After it ends someone asks, *Was that the end of the world* but his lover replies *We're all still here*. Then they all discuss the merits of the film: its cinematography, its obvious but still moving allusions to the story of Christ balanced nicely against its use of profanity and other vulgarities. Throughout the cathedral whenever someone strikes up a conversation with a new person, they will exchange the cigarettes they're smoking and both say *Wherever two or more are gathered, there you are*. The Poet sits alone in the pews. Whenever anyone decides to come and ask The Poet directly *where in this cathedral is the end of the world*, The Poet will rise, kiss the asker on the lips and whisper *And also with you*.

Acknowledgements

The titles of the following poems were taken from tweets by the account @MagicRealismBot:

A tired king constructs a shopping mall that is filled with existence
The moon is reading the communist manifesto in a labyrinth
A poet listens to a harp that plays the music of optimism
You discover you are a prime number in human form
A professor of English literature finds out that she does not exist
A trumpet suddenly appears beside you. A nun says: "This is the end."
A queen passes a law against consciousness
There is a tulip in the Garden of Eden that feels clean.
A poet steals the end of the world and hides it inside a cathedral

I am deeply grateful to the editors of the following journals for publishing the following poems that appear in this book:

"A poet steals the end of the world and hides it inside a cathedral" - Defunkt
"The Gospel According to My 3am Drunk Texts" – Sonoran Review
"A professor of English literature finds out that she does not exist" - Dream Pop
"Every day I eat one cloud from the sky" - Petrichor
"A poem made entirely of questions" - Vagabond City
"It's easier to write poetry about dead things" - Night Coffee Lit.
"Created Myth" - Hobart After Dark
"How my father did not say goodbye"- Indianapolis Review
"A tired king constructs a shopping mall that is filled with existence"- Gordon Square Review
"The summer I didn't kill myself (and every summer since)"- Stone of Madness Press
"On occasion of my own death" – Flypaper Lit
"In the future I will live on the moon"- mutiny!
"February in Ohio"- the journal of american language
"Elegy to bees" - Honey & Lime

Thank you so much to Couri Johnson for believing in this book and giving it a home.

Thank you to Hilary Plum, Mary Biddinger, Jennifer Mercer, and especially Caryl Pagel. Teachers and mentors who helped shape me as a writer and shape this collection.

Thank you to Ross Gay and Hanif Abdurraqib for your beautiful writing and for the generosity you've each shown whenever I've had the chance to speak with you.

Thank you to the many writers whom I've never met whose work inspires me: Paige Lewis, Mathias Svalina, Natalie Shapero, Kaveh Akbar, Bridgit Pegeen Kelly, Danez Smith, Franny Choi, Tommy Pico, Zach Little, Phoebe Bridgers, and Francis Quinlan to name a few.

Thank you to Noor for love, friendship, vulnerability, accountability, laughter, shared pettiness, generosity in sharing your writing and reading mine, and so much more. I am so grateful to share a home with you.

To my writing family: Lara, Threa, Fargo, George, Zach P., Danny, Gabby, David & Jesse. You are beautiful. Your words are beautiful. I'm so glad to know you all.

To Rex & G. Thank you for often being two of my first—and always two of my best—readers.

To Mom and Dad. I miss you both so much every day. I wish you could hold this book in your hands. Thank you for life and everything else.

To Annie, Mariam B., Reema, Salma, Marla, Mariam R. Mariam A., Wilson, Ayah, Zaza, Jacob, Jazz, Em, Dee, Kate, Alex, Sal, Moss, Zach B., Cody, EdNick, Aunt Barbara and all of my other loves—thank you. A million times, thank you.

About the Author

Delilah McCrea is a trans, anarchist poet living in Dearborn, Michigan. She loves the NBA and knows the lyrics to every Saintseneca song. *The Book of Flowers* is her debut poetry collection. More of her work can be found at dtmccrea.wordpress.com/